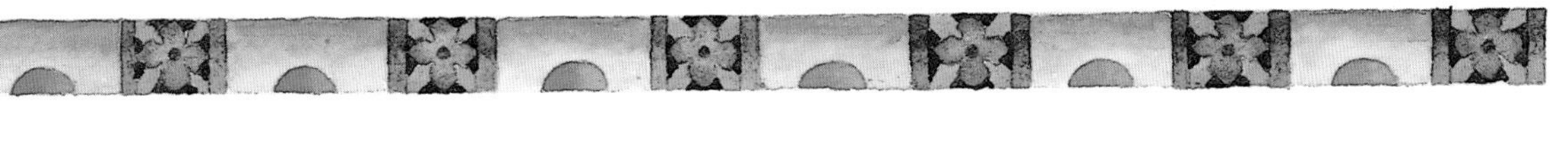

THE VOICE

THE VOICE

a sequence of poems by Walter de la Mare
chosen and illustrated by
Catherine Brighton

Published by Delacorte Press
1 Dag Hammarskjold Plaza
New York, N.Y. 10017

This work was originally published in Great Britain by Faber and Faber Limited.

Manufactured in Great Britain

First printing

Library of Congress Cataloging-in-Publication Data

De la Mare, Walter, 1873–1956.
The voice.
Poems.
Summary: An illustrated collection of thirteen
poems, describing both quiet scenes from daily life
and fanciful flights of the imagination.
1. Children's poetry, English. [1. English poetry]
I. Brighton, Catherine, ill. II. Title.
PR6007.E3V6 1986 821'.912 86–16640
ISBN 0–385–29532–4

Rain

I woke in the swimming dark
And heard, now sweet, now shrill,
The voice of the rain-water,
    Cold and still,

Endlessly sing; now faint,
In the distance borne away;
Now in the air float near,
    But nowhere stay;

Singing I know not what,
Echoing on and on;
Following me in sleep,
    Till night was gone.

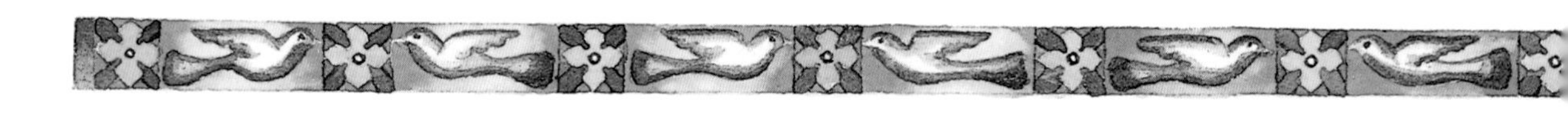

Tiny Eenanennika

Tiny Eenanennika
Was like a little bird;
If the least whisper sounded,
She heard, oh, she heard!
Claw or wing, in bush or brake,
However soft it stirred.

Tiny Eenanennika
Had bright gold hair;
Fair as a field of wheat,
Like sunshine, fair,
Like flame, like gilded water – oh,
Past words to declare!

And every sing-song bird there is,
Titmouse to wren,
In springtime, in nesting-time,
Would watch keep; and when
She chanced to look the other way
Would steal up, and then –

Snip from her shining head
Just one hair, or twain,
A gleaming, glistening, shimmering thread,
And fly off again –
A gossamer of glittering gold,
And flit off again.

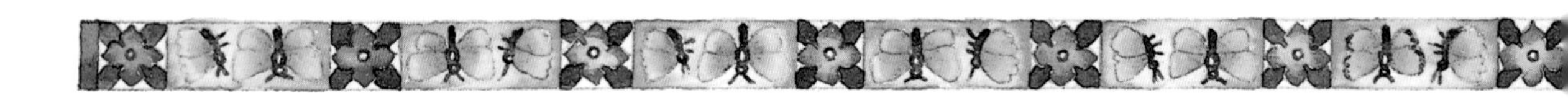

The Double

I curtseyed to the dovecote.
I curtseyed to the well.
I twirled me round and round about,
The morning scents to smell.
When out I came from spinning so,
Lo, betwixt green and blue
Was the ghost of me – a fairy child –
A-dancing – dancing, too.

Nought was of her wearing
That is the earth's array.
Her thistledown feet beat airy fleet,
Yet set no blade astray.
The gossamer shining dews of June
Showed grey against the green;
Yet never so much as a bird-claw print
Of footfall to be seen.

Fading in the mounting sun,
That image soon did pine.
Fainter than moonlight thinned the locks
That shone as clear as mine.
Vanished! Vanished! O, sad it is
To spin and spin – in vain;
And never to see the ghost of me
A-dancing there again.

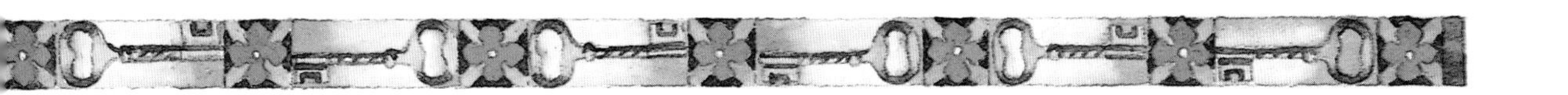

The Cupboard

I know a little cupboard,
With a teeny tiny key,
And there's a jar of Lollipops
For me, me, me.

It has a little shelf, my dear,
As dark as dark can be,
And there's a dish of Banbury Cakes
For me, me, me.

I have a small fat grandmamma,
With a very slippery knee,
And she's Keeper of the Cupboard,
With the key, key, key.

And when I'm very good, my dear,
As good as good can be,
There's Banbury Cakes, and Lollipops
For me, me, me.

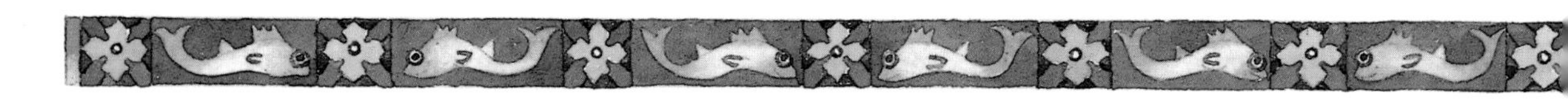

Tartary

If I were Lord of Tartary,
  Myself, and me alone,
My bed should be of ivory,
  Of beaten gold my throne;
And in my court should peacocks flaunt,
And in my forests tigers haunt,
And in my pools great fishes slant
    Their fins athwart the sun.

If I were Lord of Tartary,
  Trumpeters every day
To all my meals should summon me,
  And in my courtyards bray;
And in the evening lamps should shine,
Yellow as honey, red as wine,
While harp, and flute, and mandoline
    Made music sweet and gay.

If I were Lord of Tartary,
  I'd wear a robe of beads,
White, and gold, and green they'd be –
  And small and thick as seeds;
And ere should wane the morning star,
I'd don my robe and scimitar,
And zebras seven should draw my car
    Through Tartary's dark glades.

Lord of the fruits of Tartary,
  Her rivers silver-pale!
Lord of the hills of Tartary,
  Glen, thicket, wood and dale!
Her flashing stars, her scented breeze,
Her trembling lakes, like foamless seas,
Her bird-delighting citron-trees,
    In every purple vale!

The Voice

As I sat in the gloaming
I heard a voice say,
Weep no more, sigh no more;
Come, come away!

It was dusk at the window;
From down in the street
No rumble of carts came,
No passing of feet.

I sat very still,
Too frightened to play;
And again the voice called me,
Little boy, come away!

Dark, darker it grew;
Stars came out, and the moon
Shone clear through the glass
The carpet upon.

I listened and listened;
But no more would it say –
The voice that had called me,
Come, come away!

The Old Stone House

Nothing on the grey roof, nothing on the brown,
Only a little greening where the rain drips down;
Nobody at the window, nobody at the door,
Only a little hollow which a foot once wore;
But still I tread on tiptoe, still tiptoe on I go,
Past nettles, porch, and weedy well, for oh, I know
A friendless face is peering, and a clear still eye
Peeps closely through the casement as my step goes by.

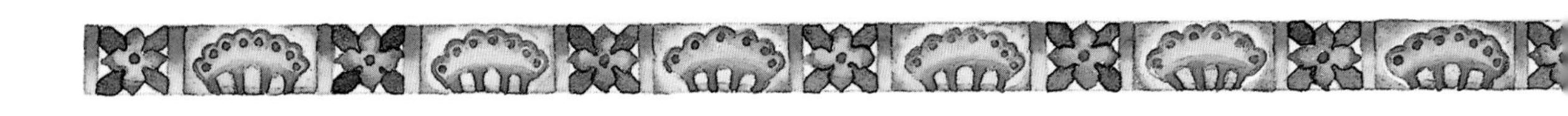

The Comb

My mother sate me at her glass;
This necklet of bright flowers she wove;
Crisscross her gentle hands did pass,
And wound in my hair her love.

Deep in the mirror our glances met,
And grieved, lest from her care I roam,
She kissed me through her tears, and set
On high this spangling comb.

Coals

In drowsy fit
I hear the flames
Syllabling o'er
Their ancient names:
The coals – a glory
Of gold – blaze on,
Drenched with the suns
Of centuries gone;
While, at the window,
This rainy day
In darkening twilight
Dies away.

Ice

The North Wind sighed:
And in a trice
What was water
Now is ice.

What sweet rippling
Water was
Now bewitched is
Into glass:

White and brittle
Where is seen
The prisoned milfoil's
Tender green;

Clear and ringing,
With sun aglow,
Where the boys sliding
And skating go.

Now furred's each stick
And stalk and blade
With crystals out of
Dewdrops made.

Worms and ants,
Flies, snails and bees
Keep close house-guard,
Lest they freeze;

Oh, with how sad
And solemn an eye
Each fish stares up
Into the sky.

In dread lest his
Wide watery home
At night shall solid
Ice become.

Snow

No breath of wind,
No gleam of sun –
Still the white snow
Whirls softly down –
Twig and bough
And blade and thorn
All in an icy
Quiet, forlorn.
Whispering, rustling,
Through the air,
On sill and stone,
Roof – everywhere,
It heaps its powdery
Crystal flakes,
Of every tree
A mountain makes;
Till pale and faint
At shut of day,
Stoops from the West
One wintry ray.
And, feathered in fire,
Where ghosts the moon,
A robin shrills
His lonely tune.

Mistletoe

Sitting under the mistletoe
(Pale-green, fairy mistletoe),
One last candle burning low,
All the sleepy dancers gone,
Just one candle burning on,
Shadows lurking everywhere:
Some one came, and kissed me there.

Tired I was; my head would go
Nodding under the mistletoe
(Pale-green, fairy mistletoe);
No footsteps came, no voice, but only,
Just as I sat there, sleepy, lonely,
Stooped in the still and shadowy air
Lips unseen – and kissed me there.

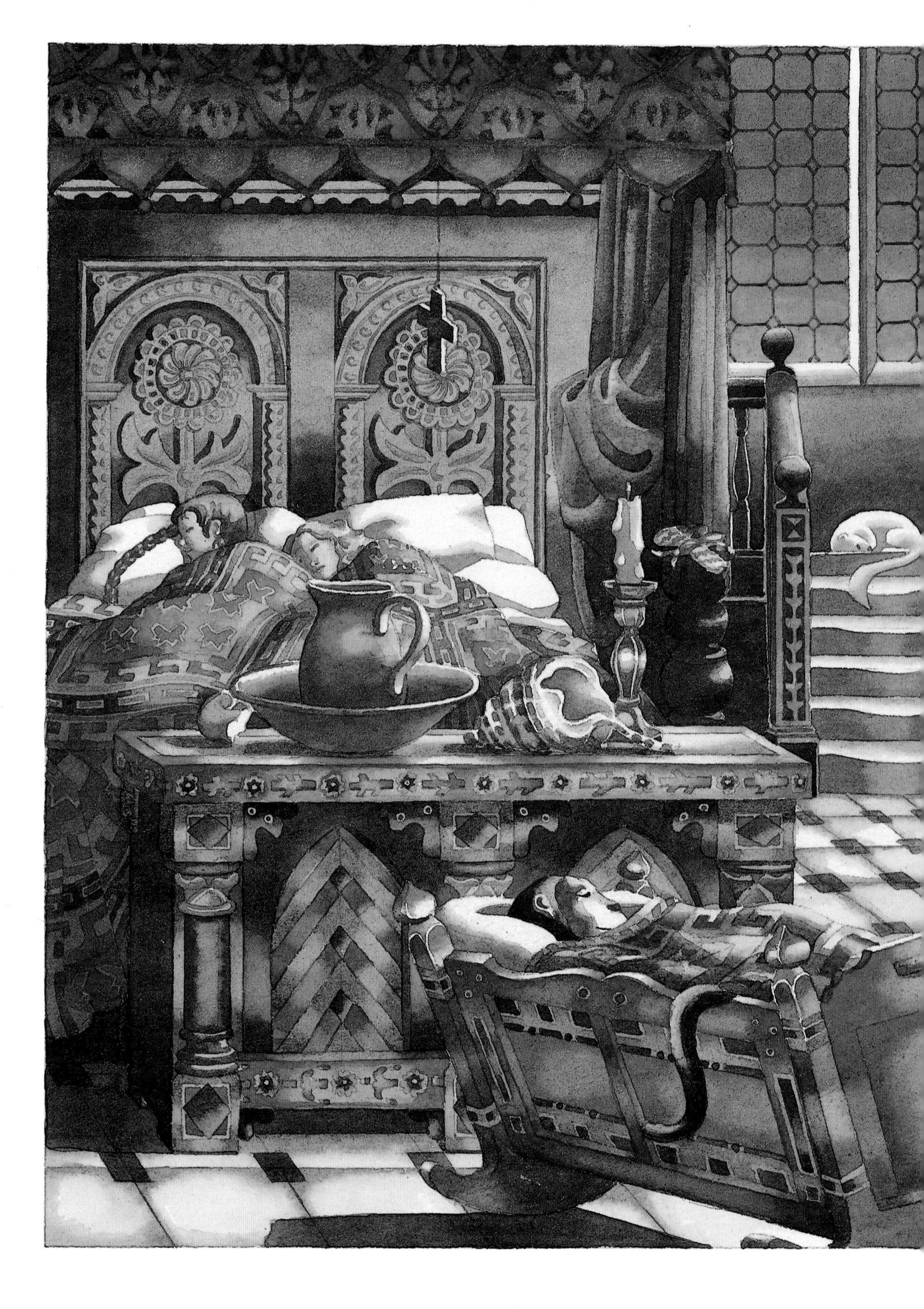

Asleep

Sister with sister, dark and fair,
Slumber on one pillow there;
Tranced in dream their phantoms rove –
But none knows what they are dreaming of.
Lost to the room they love, they lie
Their hearts their only lullaby.
Whither that cloud in heaven is bound
Can neither tell. No scent, no sound
Reaches them now. Without avail
Warbles the sweet-tongued nightingale.
Oh, how round, how white a moon
Streams into this silent room!
Clothes and curtains gleam so gay
        It might be day.
But see, beyond that door ajar,
        Night's shadows are;
And not a mouse is stirring where
        Descends an empty stair.